Three One Act Plays

To Kathleen

Peter Routis

PETER ROUTIS

ISBN 978-1-64569-580-6 (paperback)
ISBN 978-1-64569-581-3 (digital)

Christian Faith Publishing, Inc.
832 Park Avenue
Meadville, PA 16335
www.christianfaithpublishing.com

Printed in the United States of America

For Johanna and Theodore who deserved better.

"I know that each one of us travels to love alone,
alone to faith and to death. I know it. I've tried
it. It doesn't help. Let me come with you."

Giannis Ritsos, 20th century Poet

The Tragedy of Job

THE CHARACTERS

Moses
Abraham
Samuel
David
Nehemiah
Prince of Darkness
The Voice of God
Chorus: (four women of Uz)
Chorus Leader
Mathousalla
Job
Job's Wife
Eliphaz
Bildad
Zophar

SCENE 1

(The stage lights are dim. The stage is empty. Motionless clouds appear here and there. As the lights become brighter, one can see Moses, Abraham, Samuel, David, Nehemiah, and the Prince of Darkness standing, talking to each other quietly, but not the Prince of Darkness.)

THE VOICE OF GOD. (*Offstage.*) My beloved children. It has been some time since our last gathering. However, earthly concerns have kept us away from each other. Now that we all gathered here, it's time we address the actions of feeble-minded and thoughtless men who have shown their disrespect and dishonour to our heavenly kingdom. I will start with you, Prince of Darkness. Tell us, where have you been and what were your observations?

PRINCE OF DARKNESS. My lord, first, I would like to express my gratitude toward your lordship and assure you of my obedience and loyalty to you. I have spent a lot of time with the people down on earth, wandering among them, observing their simple daily lives. Life indeed is very hard for a lot of humans, working as hard as they can, ploughing the earth, guiding their sheep and goats to their pastures, caring for their families. My heart is very…

THE VOICE OF GOD. (*Interrupting.*) Prince of Darkness, it has come to my attention that you observed our servant Job very intensely and unnecessarily.

PRINCE OF DARKNESS. I observed our servant Job with kindness but with suspicion. His evil thoughts have run across all aspects of life, including his.

THE VOICE OF GOD. Have you not considered our servant Job as the most perfect and righteous man? Have you not considered his fear of me and of evil?

PRINCE OF DARKNESS. My lord, do you perhaps believe that the fear he has of you is not justified? Didn't you help him obtain the wealth that he enjoys? Seven sons, three daughters, seven thousand sheep, three thousand camels, five hundred yoke of oxen, five hundred asses, servants, attendants, lands…

THE VOICE OF GOD, (*interrupting*). He has obtained all his wealth with my help, yes. But do you dismiss his own efforts and hard work? What else have you to say, our beloved son?

PRINCE OF DARKNESS. And you, my lord, you think that he will let you touch anything he owns, I suppose?

THE VOICE OF GOD. And you, my son, do you believe your clever presentation and accusations will persuade me to abandon my true servant?

PRINCE OF DARKNESS. No. But I will tell you this. Put your hand forward and attempt to touch his wealth. He will curse you and…

THE VOICE OF GOD. (*Interrupting.*) I made him and I will destroy him. If what you say is true, I place all the power in your hands. Go and prove to me that your accusations are true. I will be waiting for your return. (*The Prince of Darkness exits, stage right.*)

(*The lights go out for a few moments. When the lights come on, all remain in their positions as before. The Prince of Darkness enters, stage right.*)

THE VOICE OF GOD. (*Heard offstage.*) You have travelled very far indeed to bring me the news which I'm already familiar with. You have not proven to me his greediness and his unfaithfulness. Before I speak of my decision about your wrong accusations of an innocent man, what have you lastly to say? You have partly destroyed him without any cause. I will never forgive you.

PRINCE OF DARKNESS. My lord, he has bones and flesh, blood running in his veins, and his mind is as sound as that of a young man. But if you attempt to touch his flesh or his bones, he will curse you. Let me go and prove that to you.

THE VOICE OF GOD. Go, but spare his life. This uncertainty and false accusations of a faithful servant to me has upset me a great deal. Go, and I will wait for your return. (*Prince of Darkness exits, stage right. The lights go out.*)

SCENE 2

(A tree far stage right. In the background, healthy fields can be seen, and beyond the fields, one can see the mountains of Shiloh. Job enters stage left. Walks slowly toward the tree and sits down.)

JOB. (*Soliloquy.*)
>I died last night
>The time of silence
>In the kingdom of yellow and red flowers
>And I woke up with the first kiss of the sea
>With down
>To live a day of charity, with a superhuman respect
>To reach the sun as if I were already human.
>And then, in the endless night, where the waters meet the pebbles
>Under the silver sphere of the moon
>I got a hold of my life setting among yellow trees
>Of the silent slope, loaded with the leaves of the beech tree.
>Innumerable hands carry me away
>Under the bubbling of the empty moments
>Of the leaves of dew!
>It's dawning. Ashes of the event
>Deadly shapes which try to process the fibres of the day
>Let me be young again and free
>Among haughty cypresses and pine trees
>To race my wishes through the white temples
>And nothing I would care more for
>Than the sky and the earth
>Which allow me to run with my naked feet

Among the trees
And the friendly winds of my thoughts.
And then, it was blue and yellow and green
As in a dream
And the heart was long of the trees as the sun was
born over and over
Among the legs and the bosoms of the nymphs…
The clouds, the fibres of the day.
And then, to awake, and the fields and the mountains
Like the shadows of the moonlight
With the silent wind which caresses my face
It was all peaceful and blue and grey
As I saw my shadow chasing the sun
Which grew smaller that very moment.
So, it must have been the birth of the simple light
In the island of the nymphs
"Lady of the Wild Things," as she was called,
And being loved among deer and doves
In the green endless fields
Under the golden stars.
Let me be the shepherd once more
And my wishes will race through the notes of my fife
And my tears through the mountains.
It was blue and green
As the morning song raised from the petals of my
eyes
Wet with the morning dew and red from the chains
of my youth
I will recall time and time again
As I run my pathos up my naked eyes.
And the grass was green and blue was the sea
Under the white and grey sky and I was running
down the hill
As when I was a boy, with the smile in my red lips
And the hope and love at the side of my eye.
The yellow flowers

Among the leaves of the green grass
Were caressing my naked feet
And my open, hairless chess was resisting the wind
Under the sun which was born that very moment.
I was famous among the trees! And I was happy and
carefree
As I was left in the mercy of the winds
Let me be free once again
And sing as the fields were home
And the sounds from the mountains were mine.
Nothing I cared more than
The moon of the sea which rose from its waters
And it was getting dark and grey
As I was dying young and easy;
Though, I sang through my tears, like the sea.
I was born only once, as the moon rises only once
Young and red, dipped in the mercy of the land.
Nothing I cared more than the night of my death
When everything will be green and white
And the sea will be singing my hymn
Under the sun
Which will be born that very moment;
I will celebrate the event of my existence
Only once
Running down the hill, where the sun will grow
round, once again
And time will allow me wishes, raised through the
fields of green
Before it takes them away, under the shadow of my
hand
In the moonlight
As I ride, forever, to sleep.

(Job gets up, and slowly starts his exit stage left. He stops, he looks toward the mountains and the fields, puts his head down, and exits. Lights go out.)

SCENE 3

(Slowly the lights illuminate the stage. The Prince of Darkness enters with an evil smile in his face. He looks behind him. There is a fire far away of a big field. Noises of men and animals are heard offstage. He turns toward the audience and speaks with passion but very powerfully.)

PRINCE OF DARKNESS. (*Soliloquy.*)

I open my mouth and the whole world trembles, and it carries my words to its darkest caves…and whispers them gently to the innocent, foolish men who weep in the night over their troubles. I carve my veins and the dreams turn red to become hoops in the children's alleys, and sheets for the girls lying awake, secretly listening to the marvels of God. Dizzy with human whispers, I go down to the valley and bury the bodies of my secret dead and cut the golden cord of their betrayed stars so they may fall free into the black abyss. The iron turns rusty and I punish its century. I, who suffered the myriad, piercing points of my darkness out of fire and sulphur, I fashion a new knife fit for heroes. I bare my breasts and the winds are unleashed. They sweep away ruins and broken souls and clear the earth of its murky clouds so to revel the meadows of bliss. (*Exits stage right. Lights go out.*)

SCENE 4

CHORUS. (*The lights illuminate the stage. The stage is empty except for a tree, stage right. On the back ground a burning field is seen and the wind makes waves of it. The chorus enters stage left.*)

My foundations on the mountains and the people carry the mountains on their shoulders, and on these mountains, memory burns like the unconsumed bush. Memory of my people, they call you Moses, and they call you David. Time is in turmoil and hangs the day by its feet, emptying the bones of the humbled with a sudden clatter. Who, how, when did they climb the abyss? Which, whose, how many armies? The face of the sky turns and my enemies have gone far away. Memory of my people, they call you Abraham, and they call you Isaak. You alone know the stone's cutting edge. It is you who sharpens the feature of our prophets, to the rim of our eternal waters. You touch my mind and it hurts the infant of spring. You punish my hand and it turns whiter in the darkness. You always pass through fire to reach brightness. You always pass through brightness to reach the top haloed mountains. But what are the mountains? Who and what are on the mountains? My foundations on the mountains and the people carry the mountains on their shoulders, and on those mountains, memory burns like the unconsumed bush.

CHORUS LEADER, (*enters stage left*).

Hold your tongues and look at the disaster which has fallen upon our good servant, Job. (*The chorus moves towards Job who's sleeping under the tree dreaming and smiling.*) Look how peaceful he sleeps and how happy he looks

15

under this olive tree. Do not wake him yet for he will sink into the darkness of despair of what has happened to him. (*The chorus and the chorus leader sit by Job quietly.*)

MATHOUSALLA, (*enters stage left and approaches Job who is still asleep*).

My lord, my lord, catastrophe has fallen upon our heads.

JOB (*sitting up, rubbing his eyes*). Who's uttering catastrophe and disturbed my sleep?

MATHOUSALLA, (*interrupting*).

My lord, as the oxen were plowing and the asses feeding beside them, the Sabeans fell upon them and took them away. But that was not enough. They massacred all the servants with their swords and only I survived.

JOB, (*stands up, raises his hands upwards toward the heavens*).

Oh, ho, ho. Is that a curse you dissented upon my head my lord? Is that a curse which signifies your displeasure with me? (*Job falls to his knees.*)

MATHOUSALLA.

My lord, God sent fire from the heavens and has burnt all the sheep and the fields. The Chaldeans forming three bands fell upon the camels taking them away. Your sons and daughters were gathered around the table for supper at your oldest son's house when a great wind came from the wilderness and swept them away not to be seen again.

JOB, (*speaks quietly and soberly*).

Naked, I came out of my mother's womb, and naked I will return. The Lord gave me all my wealth, and the lord will take it away. Blessed be the name of the Lord.

CHORUS.

The creator of clouds, mountains, seas, and men sleeps inside me. His dark lips always on the hurricane's nipple and his soul always in the seas, kick against the mountain's shin.

JOB'S WIFE (*entering stage right, speaking loudly with agitation*).

Do you still retain your integrity after all this? Curse God and die.

JOB.

Alas, woman. You speak as foolish women do. Are we to receive only good from God and not evil? But hold your irrational tongue. My friends are coming.

(*Eliphaz, Bildad, and Zophar enter stage left. They all sit down, looking very sober.*)

JOB (*raises his hands and speaks with grief*).

Let the day perish wherein I was born. Alas, let the stars of the twilight be dark and never see the dawning of the day. Why didn't I die from the womb?

ELIPHAZ.

Why, Job? What happened to your strength? Were you not the one who used to strengthen the weak hands and feeble knees? Why can't you control your own weakness and strengthen yourself? What happened to your confidence, your hope, and your fears of God?

THE VOICE OF GOD, (*the voice is heard offstage*).

Will mortal man be more just than God? Will a man be more pure than his creator? Men are nothing. Job, you are nothing. God made you and God will destroy you as he destroyed a lot of men who died without wisdom.

JOB.

Oh, that my grief were thoroughly weighed and my calamity laid in the balances together. For now it would be heavier, my words are swallowed up. What is my strength that I should hope for? What is my end that I should prolong my life? Is my strength the strength of stone? Is my flesh of brass? Now be content and look upon me. Return, I implore you, let it not be iniquity and return again my righteousness. Is there iniquity in my tongue? Can't my taste discern perverse things? Now, my Lord, I will not refrain my mouth. I will speak in the anguish of my spirit;

I will complain in the bitterness of my soul. When I say, my bed comforts me and my couch eases my complaints, you frighten me with dreams so that my soul chooses strangling and death rather than my life. (*Lights go out.*)

CHORUS, (*sitting around and under the tree*).

I turn my eyes full of tears toward the window and gazing out at the burned trees of the valley, I said, "Sisters, even these will get justice one day." I bit into the day; not a single drop of green blood dripped. I shouted at the gates of God and my voice took the grief of murderers. In the earth's centre appeared the Prince of Darkness, growing darker and darker, and the sun's rays, look, became the guiding threads of death.

CHORUS LEADER.

Oh, bitter women dressed in black, virgins, and mothers. You who gave water at the fountain to the angel's nightingales, even you were given, by the Prince of Darkness himself, your handful of fate. Out of the wells you now draw cries of those unjustly killed.

BILDAD.

Job, my good friend, and you, women of Uz, how long will you speak of these things? If your children have sinned and you are pure and upright, our good Lord will not forget that and he will give justice. Our father will not cast away a perfect man. They who hate him will be clothed with shame.

JOB.

He is wise in heart and mighty in strength, but how much less will I answer him and choose out my words to reason with him? If I justify myself, my own mouth will condemn me. If I say I am perfect, it will also prove me perverse. But I know my days are few. Take your leave and let me alone so I can take some comfort. I will go and I will not return, neither to the land of darkness nor to the shadow of death.

ZOPHAR.

Our Lord knows the vain men. He sees wickedness as well. If you prepare your heart and stretch out your hand toward him, then he will forget your misery.

JOB, (*speaks with agitation*).

Enough, my vicious consolers. I have heard many such things. You are all miserable comforters. Vain words do not have an end. My witness is in heaven and my record is on high. When my time comes, I will die, but now, I am innocent. (*Job walks toward the tree, touches its torso, feels it, looks up in the sky, smiles a bitter smile, places his hand on his heart, and soliloquizes.*) My breath is corrupt, my days are extinct. The graves are ready for me. Are they mocking me? He that speaks flattery to his friends, the eyes of his children will fail. My eyes are dim by reason of sorrow. But, no, my heart. You are innocent. Upright men will be astonished at this injustice and the innocent will stir up himself against the hypocrite. But as for my friends, I cannot find one wise man among them. My days are past. Alas. My purpose is broken off. Alas. Even the thoughts of my heart. Alas. Alas. Alas. They change the day into night. The light is short because of darkness. If I wait, the grave is my house. I have made my bed in the darkness, but first, I will speak to him.

CHORUS.

With the lantern of the stars, I went out into heaven. How in the frost of the meadows, the world's only shore, can I find my soul? Weeping myrtle, silver with sleep, sprinkled my face, I blow and go alone. How can I find my soul? Leader of rays and the creator of the universe, vagabond who knows the future, speak to me. How can I find my soul? Nights with a hundred hands stir my entrails throughout the firmament. This pain burns. How can I find my soul? With the star's lantern, I roam the heavens in the frost of the meadows, the world's only shore. How can I find my soul, the four-leaf tear!

19

JOB, (*appears at the top of the mountain. It's dark and late at night.*)

My lord, I came here tonight in the mist on top of the mountain to talk to you. My complaint is bitter tonight. My stroke is heavier than my groaning. Will you plead against me with your great power? There, the righteous might dispute with you, so should I be delivered forever from my judge? My feet have held your footsteps and I kept your way and I did not decline. Neither have I gone back from the commandments of your lips. I have esteemed the words of your mouth more than my necessary food. You made my heart and you troubled it.

CHORUS.

The night blew and the houses went out and it's late inside my soul. No one hears me whether I knock, and memory kills me. He said, "My brothers, black hours are near, time will tell. The joys of men have soiled the guts of monsters." I turn my eyes full of tears toward heaven. I shout at the gates of God and my voice took on the grief of murderers, and in the earth's centre, a black phantom that looks like the Prince of Darkness, appeared growing darker and darker and the sun's rays, look, became the guiding thread of death.

VOICE OF GOD, (*the voice is heard with echo and Job looks frightened*).

Who is this who darken my words without knowledge? Where were you when I laid the foundations of this world? Who has laid the measures thereof? Who shut up the sea with doors?

JOB (*fearful*).

My Lord, I know you can do anything and that no thought can be withheld from you. I have heard you with my ears. Now, I can see you with my heart.

VOICE OF GOD.

My blessing to you my good servant, Job. My wrath is kindled against Eliphaz and against your two friends, for they have not spoken of me the things that are right as you have. So take unto you seven bullocks and seven rams and offer up for them a burnt offering and pray for them.

CHORUS. (*Gradually during this speech, the lights go out and a spot light gradually illuminates the chorus.*)

This world, this world is one and the same world of suns and dust of turmoil and quiet evenings, weaver of constellations, silver gilder of moss, at the warning of memory and the exit of dreams. This world, this world is one and the same world. Soaring above floods, plunging under typhoons by night with the syrinx, by day with the lyre, on the cobblestones of cities, the jib-sails of meadows. Flat-headed, long-headed, willing, unwilling, both Solomon and the son of Haggith. This world, this world is one and the same world of ebbing and orgasm of remorse and clouding. Inventor of zodiacs, daredevil of domes at the rim of the ecliptic at the farthest reach of creation. This world, this world is one and the same world. It is both brass sounding brass and a vain distant cloud! (*The spotlight remains for a few moments on the chorus. Brief tableau. The lights dim and slowly go out.*)

The Tragedy of Eli

THE CHARACTERS

Narrator
Eli: (priest and prophet of Israel)
Samuel: (later prophet of Israel)
Elkanah: (Samuel's father)
Hannah: (Samuel's mother)
Servants (of Elkanah and Hannah)
Voice of God of Israel
Young Boy (serves Eli)
1st Messenger (soldier from the army of Israelites)
2nd Messenger (soldier from the army of Israelites)

(A long table in the middle of the stage with two benches at either side. In the background, we see fields and beyond the fields the mountains of Shiloh. The narrator enters and stands stage left under a spotlight.)

NARRATOR.

One more day ends as the sun hides behind the western hills of Shiloh. One more day in the unbearable childless misery of Hannah. One more day, and the yearly sacrifice of three bullocks by Hannah and Elkanah will take place again at the temple outside Eli's house.

The leaves of the trees have turned yellow and light autumn rain falls upon the dry land, as seasons change and winter is on its way. But it's cold and grey and dull as in the bitter heart of Hannah.

Thirteen years have passed. Thirteen years of prayers and sacrifices. Thirteen years of anticipation and vows. But who can doubt God's power and mercifulness? We believe in the God of Israel; we believe in the divine power of the king of our land. We believe in him; in our Saviour.

But here she comes. With tears carving her face, Hannah walks slowly, followed by her husband and our lord Eli. Will our God pity her and give her the much-desired son that she wishes so much?

Come, sorrowful autumn, and you, white winter, for we wait for spring to bring us hope. May the rebirth of nature be the birth of her happiness!

(The spot light goes out. The Narator exits. The lights come on to illuminate the entire stage. Enter Hannah, Elkanah, Eli, and the Young Boy.)

ELKANAH *(to Hannah)*.

Come now, Hannah. Your eyes haven't dried for days and your tormented soul bows to the sadness you feel in your heart. Come, sit here, *(pointing to the bench in front of the table)*. Let's eat, for our trip was long and the relentless rain didn't light up until we got here. Today is a day of happiness. We waited the entire year for this event. The temple is ready for the sacrifice and our beloved host, Eli, has done all the preparations for the event. My heart is exulted and my spirit is flying high up to reach the Lord. (*They all sit on the bench in front of the table. The table is set with food, wine, and plates. Elkanah places a plate in front of Hannah.*) Crying is only the outcry of a sad and desperate heart. You must always hope, for our God is omnipotent.

ELI. Eat my child and don't let yourself be neglected.

HANNAH (*sober*). I must pray.

ELKANAH. We will pray together

HANNAH. I will pray alone. I have things to tell him.

(*Hannah gets up and walks toward stage left front. Both hands in front of her chest and she stands gazing ahead. Eli, Elkanah, and the Young Boy are talking silently at the table.*)

HANNAH.

Here I am before you, with my troubled soul dedicated to you as my heart groans under your wings. The years, one after the other, have passed, as we slain for you three bullocks every time. I see their blood running down the temple, and I pray for it to reach you. Pity me and give me my son. The winter comes and I darken. The spring comes and I hope. Give me a son and before he reaches the sixth year of his age, he will be yours again. I will bring him here at this temple, and he will serve you until you take him away. His hair will never be touched by a razor and he will be as pure as the waters of our mountain springs.

(*Hannah walks toward the table and sits down. They all start eating except Hannah. She sits quietly.*)

ELI, (*offering her a cup of wine*).

> Here's for your sorrow. Give thanks to our Lord to soothe your troubled soul.

HANNAH.

> No, my lord. Neither wine nor any strong spirits will restore my bitter heart. I'm a woman of sorrow and my soul is set by God. Weakness has a long way to reach me, for I am a handmaid with manners. Though my heart is heavy from my complaints and I have spoken to him.

ELI.

> May peace come to your soul, my child, and your demands may be answered and fulfil your bitter heart.

(*Lights go out. The lights go on again at the far end stage left where Hannah stands.*)

HANNAH, (*soliloquy*).

> The night is restless, covered with a profound darkness. My entire body, soul, and spirit are burning all at once under the thoughts of my sterility. And the stars, as if they are wandering travellers in the Negev desert, are drowned and disappear in the endless dark chaos…as I'm kneeling under the heavenly vault, praying, and I groan and in the holy silence of the night, my sigh is heard, as we hear Moses calling the God of Israel. It is not a dream, neither is it dark thoughts of the night, but the endless conflict which bursts out of the depths of my soul, flowing in my veins, travelling on that endless road, asking, "Why? Why should I trouble my mind with inexistent thoughts? Why should I analyze every little thought which seems so clear with the clarity of the waters of a mountain spring? Why should I doubt? If I could, I would embrace with the wings of my soul everything I feel. If I could, I would feel everything. He murmurs to me silently, covered with the veil of honesty, away from doubt and the limits of non-existence, away from the nets of desperation

and agony, away from the strong wind of disappointment, beyond the limits of nothingness. If I could, I would see with the doubles eyes of my soul his existence and halt the agony which has tormented my soul." I have been granted my wish. My heart is rejoicing because I have conceived. I have conceived my much desired son, and he is his. He is his and what remains is happiness. The night is coming slowly, liturgically, from the petals of the rosebush, as the stars pop out of the heavenly vault resembling hope. And it was night, warm, tender, and it was the winnowed of the night which was heard in the eternal silence…and it was time for rejoicing.

(*The lights go out. When they come on again, it reveals Eli's house. Two beds of straw and a table with two benches. Samuel, now a young man, walking slowly from left to right, reading. Eli enters stage left and sits on a bench, looking at Samuel, who keeps on reading. A smile forms on Eli's face.*)

Eli, (*smiling*).

I suppose, my child, learning to read is like learning to walk. It's a new concept which only a few people have mastered. (*Samuel stops reading and looks at Eli*). Now that you are working with me, you must read and read continuously. A lot of writing has been left by our forefathers, and we must teach our people the truth. But come now, finish your lesson. The sun will soon reach its zenith. (*Samuel smiles. Eli looks at Samuel, reflects, and smiling he gets up.*) Oh, of course, of course, my child. I know why you're so happy today. Your parents are coming for the sacrifice. Three bullocks every year; three bullocks we slain for the sake of eternity.

Samuel, (*stops reading and turns to face Eli*).

For the sake of eternity. What do you mean, my lord?

ELI.

> Don't let your mind be bothered by that now. Finish your reading and get ready for the sacrifice. (*Eli goes back to the bench and sits.*)

SAMUEL, (*resumes his reading. A few moments then he raises his head. Calmly*).

> My lord, is there life after death?

ELI (*reflecting*).

> There is life after death, of course, but a different kind. Life is something you can feel. Life is called the everyday struggle and what is after death is the effects of your life. You get on the path of life and you become familiar with it. At the beginning the path is beautiful. Flowers in your path, trees above your head where you can seek shelter from the burning sun, birds flying above your head, chanting the beauty of life. You walk on this path, soliloquizing or whispering beloved poets' poems. But your path is not like that always.

SAMUEL.

> I suppose life could be wonderful, my lord, if it were built upon that path. I made a name for it. I should call it, oh, yes, I should call it, "Serene Path."

ELI.

> Oh, yes, yes, indeed. But it would be more wonderful if you built that path. God found us this land. If we neglect it, if we don't protect it, other people will come and take it away from us, like the Philistines who have tried desperately to occupy us for years. Then God will get angry and we will not be only without land and nation, but without beliefs and ideals. Then what is left for us? Slavery and another Egypt and pharaohs. But come now. You are too young to worry about that now and I am too old to talk about it. (*People talking offstage. The sounds of animals are heard.*) But what do I hear? Is my dear Hannah and Elkanah here already?

SERVANT, (*enters stage left*).

> The sun has reached high noon and the temple is ready for the sacrifice. Our beloved couple from Ramah just arrived with their three bullocks, their servants, presents, and horses. Should I ask them to come in?

ELI.

> Oh, yes, yes, indeed. Right away, my child. We shouldn't let them wait outside. I have fresh wine for them and for the libation to our God. Run now. (*The servant exits.*)

(*Hannah and Elkanah enter followed by two servants bringing presents.*)

ELI. Peace on you my child Hannah and you, Elkanah. Welcome to Shiloh.

HANNAH.

> Peace on you, too, my lord. (*Turns and looks at Samuel.*) My son, what a great pleasure to see you again. How are you? (*Embraces Samuel.*) You have grown so tall and your hair is so much longer than the last time I saw you.

SAMUEL. Hello, Mother, Father, welcome to Shiloh.

HANNAH.

> My son, I brought you your robe. This robe fills the house with your presence. Whenever I go back home after my visit here, I start making this robe, and as I get involved with it, I feel that I see you sitting right next to me.

SAMUEL.

> Come now, why are you standing here? My lord Eli has kept for you the best wine. Come sit on the bench and tell us about the Philistines.

ELI (*poring wine in the cups*). Are they still threatening us? How is our holy army?

ELKANAH.

> We are very strong. The God of our land will never allow his nation to fall into the hands of the barbarous Philistines.

ELI.

> I heard the Philistines are preparing to attack us any moment now. My sons Hophni and Phinehas are constantly armed, waiting to engage in this war, and they look so uneasy and anxious.

ELKANAH. Yes, yes, of course.

ELI.

> I pray for them and for our army every day. I have faith in our Lord. He will lead us to victory. He will never let his people fall into slavery again.

ELKANAH. People must be faithful to him too.

ELI.

> They must be. He's our king and leader after all. A flock without a leader is not a flock; a nation without a leader is not a nation.

SERVANT (*enters*). My lord

ELI. Yes, my good servant.

SERVANT.

> The temple is ready for the sacrifice. The sun is rolling slowly toward the western hills. We must start immediately.

ELI.

> Yes, we're coming. Come, my children, come. It's time to show our Lord our appreciation and keep us safe from the invaders.

(*As they exit, the lights go out, except for a light at the far stage left where the narrator stands.*)

NARRATOR.

> My heart exults in the Lord. My horn exalted in the Lord. My mouth is enlarged over my enemies. I rejoice

in your salvation. Our God, the God of Israel, is the only God, for he is the God of knowledge, and he will judge to the end of the earth, and he will give strength to his kingdom and exalt the horn of his anointed. (*Pause.*) But the night has fallen now upon our kingdom, and my lord Eli cannot sleep, for he cannot find dreams to calm his troubled spirit. He has worries in his heart. He heard of evil deeds his sons have committed. He also heard that the Philistines will attack us again. He is a misfortunate man. But here he comes. He looks very bitter, and he's a man of a sorrowful soul. Let us hear what he's hiding in his heart.

(*The lights of the rest of the stage go on where one can see the same room. Eli enters, looking very old.*)

ELI.

Alas, alas. Everything is persecuting me. Invisible powers surround my soul, as if they were the armies of Egypt. Everything has betrayed me. I have betrayed everything. Oh, armies of the spirit, oh, my soul, what more? What more dreadful than the tempest will come? I've been moulded and been put in the most beautiful form. I live and die in the most stinking mud. The first one comes from the heights of Sinai; the other is rolling down into the abyss. The sulphurous flames…the fire. Why did he give us the spirit when we let it decay useless inside us? Oh, such a dirt, such a nausea to fill man's heart. Oh, how distasteful. Who's abusing me? Who's calling me unworthy, villain? Where did my ideals go? Where did my theories go? Lies? Are all lies? How could it be? The…then…then I'm…then I'm but a hypocrite. How can I call them sons? How can I call them part of my flesh, part of my being? What are they to me? Are they not my sons? How could they betray me? Oh, happy nothingness, uncomfortable being, miserable inexistence. He came to me the other night. Yes, my Lord came to me and he set a curse upon my head and my family. Oh, my Lord, You can only destroy me. He talked of evil deeds my sons committed. He talked of destruction of my family. He called me unworthy. My house and the house of my fathers will be destroyed. He excommunicated me from his house because I deceived him. I deceived my Lord. I deceived him.

(*Eli exits stage right. Samuel enters stage left. Silence. A voice is heard offstage and Samuel raises his head to listen.*)

VOICE.

Samuel, my curse upon those who have laughed upon the unlawful sacrifices which blur the face of heaven. My curse upon the women who sleep with my young priests. My curse upon Eli and his house.

SAMUEL.

My Lord, you blew the sacred malady down upon the holy body of our lord Eli, and he falls to the ground, foaming like a snail, puffing like a turtle. Why? Why?

VOICE.

Silence. I created them and I will destroy them. They deceived me. His sons deceived me. The entire nation of Israel deceived me. I brought them from Egypt to this land, and now, they worship other gods. I will destroy the nation of Israel. I will destroy Eli and his family. Now, Samuel, listen to these words. You will be the prophet of Israel. I set my hand upon your head. Prepare yourself. Prepare yourself for the new defeat which will come upon your land. And prepare yourself for the restoration of the new Israel.

SAMUEL.

My lord, my lord. (*Samuel raises his head looking around.*) He left. He came again today to pull me from the dreadful darkness and let me hanging over the abyss. Patience and the eternal lamp will light my darkness. Life will not yield to age.

(Samuel exits, stage right. Eli and the Young Boy enter, stage left. Eli, blind now and very old, is led by the Young Boy.)

ELI. Are we in my room?

YOUNG BOY.

> In this same room, where you used to sleep so peace-fully after each day of spiritual work.

ELI. Are we alone? Is there anybody else present?

YOUNG BOY.

> How can I know that? You always told me God is with you all the time. I suppose he is here too.

ELI. Now, leave us my child. Leave us, for I have a lot of complaints to tell him.

YOUNG BOY.

> Very well, my lord, but here. Sit down on that bench behind you. Your old body cannot resist tiredness.

ELI. Yes, but my spirit and soul can resist my body. Go now but be near.

YOUNG BOY. I'm going, my lord. (*Exits stage left.*)

ELI.

> My lord. Look. My chest is heaving and blows up at the same time. I feel my heart beating my chest, and I shudder. My blood touches my heart and I groan. It touches my soul and I'm filled with a deadly agony. Give me a sign. Give me, oh, give me a command. Give me a word, a curse, or a blessing. The last one, for my people. Give me a command. That which will throw me either in the abyss or in the ascend. You fought me in the white, unprofaned temples of Shiloh. You fought me at nights. Those endless nights in my sleep, and at day, you sent me to my slow death. Your curse upon Israel burns me. I'm going around, inside the rooms of your labyrinth to find an exit. You place in my palms burning coals. I can't sleep any longer. My agony burns me. My duty suffocates my heart. The duty to my people and Israel chases me. Give me your last word. I'm at your mercy.

VOICE.

> You and your people have received my last word. My curse upon you. My curse upon, your family and the Israelites. The number of dead in the battlefield is not enough. I must create a new nation with people faithful to me.

ELI.

> My lord, we ask for mercy. Mercy for our land, mercy for our homes, mercy for our youth. Our God, our leader. Don't lead us to destruction and defeat.

1ST MESSENGER (*enters from stage left, running*).

> My lord, my lord, my tongue is bitter and my heart is heavy.

ELI. I'm here, under the clouds of defeat, in the hands of God.

1ST MESSENGER. I was looking for our prophet, Samuel.

ELI.

> Come, come now. Nothing worse can come. What happened in the battlefield? Tell me everything. What lives have been claimed and how many soldiers have fallen? What lands have the Philistines taken? My shoulders carry the curse of Israel. What you will tell me cannot be worse than that?

1ST MESSENGER.

> Israel has no more youth to fill its temples, market-places, and homes. Forty thousand men have perished and now the Philistines are masters of our land. Some men are holding what is left, but soon they will also fall.

ELI. My sons, what happened to my sons?

1ST MESSENGER.

> When I left the battlefield, they were still fighting. But now, I must go. Please inform our prophet Samuel of the events. (*1ˢᵗ Messenger exit stage left. Aging Samuel enters, stage right, with his parents, Hannah and Elkanah, both now very old. Samuel walks toward Eli.*)

SAMUEL.

> Who was that messenger who left the threshold of your home? Did he bring distressing news to you and disturbed your peace?

ELI, (*in a low and weak voice*).

> The curse of God has fallen upon our people, my child. Forty thousand soldiers have been killed and our land does not belong to us anymore.

SAMUEL.

> Have faith in him and we'll regain our beloved land. He promised me. A new land will be created, filled with honourable and faithful people.

ELI, (*covers his faces with his hands*). I'm the one to blame. My heart is heavy with the curse.

SAMUEL.

> Come now, my lord. Sit here, for you look very frail. Let it come, whatever it is. It's God's will and we cannot disobey. He created us and he will destroy us.

2ND MESSENGER, (*enters stage left, running. To Eli*).

> My lord, I have news which will make your spirit burn. Your two sons have been killed in a battle by the river, and the Philistines stole the Arc of God after occupying the temple.

ELI.

> Oh, ho, alas, that I cannot bear. The news has stirred my soul. Humans, you are made of stone. No faith, no strength, no ideals. If I had the strength and eyes, I would teach you the art of prayer so that heaven should crack.

SAMUEL. This world will never see another man as noble as this one.

HANNAH. Is that the end of our frail priest?

ELKANAH. The decline and end of our nation.

SAMUEL. The rebirth of a new nation.

2ND MESSENGER.

> My news has not been exhausted. When the wife of Phinehas heard the news, strong pains she felt inside her, and as soon as she gave birth to four sons, she died.

ELI.

She, too, paid for the curse of Israel. What a disastrous end. I have seen the world. I have seen the world and I ascended. Now I decline along with it. I'm old now and blind. No, no. No life for me, as there is no life for our nation. There is no more. But feel, feel the mountains around us. See how proud they stand. They'll stand there forever. Why life for these and not for Israel? For our blessed land. No life for our blessed land. (*Eli bends his head over his hands on the table and remains silent and motionless.*)

SAMUEL, (*bending over Eli*).

My lord, my lord, open your eyes. You have gone too far away, and I cannot reach you.

HANNAH. Let him go in peace.

ELKANAH. Heaven, I'm sure, will receive him with honour.

SAMUEL. He's gone indeed.

ELKANAH. He has endured his misfortunes far beyond the limits of human ability.

SAMUEL.

The weight of this sad time, we must obey. Speak what we feel, not what we ought to say. The old have seen a lot. We, the younger, will neither see so much nor live as long. But the years we live, we must live them with faith, for the new Israel will soon rise. (*The lights fade slowly until the stage is dark.*)

The Rats

And one step from the chaos is the abyss.

THE CHARACTERS

Old Man
Boy

(*The stage is dark. The sound of a fife flute is heard. As the lights on the stage go on, one can see a mountain slope. Rocks on stage left. A large rock on stage right. A makeshift tent made of three sticks and an old blanket stage centre. It's early in the evening. The Boy enters, stage left, limping slightly. He's in his late teens. He wears rags and a pair of old shoes, which are too small for his feet. Stops stage centre, looks toward the auditorium, turns toward stage right, reflects, looks toward stage left, reflects, looks again toward the auditorium and reflects for a while. Turns toward stage left, reflects for a second, and then takes a step toward stage left and stops. Reflects for a while, and then starts walking toward stage right. He's about to exit; stops, turns his head toward far stage nervously, looks, reflects for a moment, and then walks toward far stage, disappearing in the darkness of far stage. A few seconds. He returns to light slowly, stops at stage centre, looks down, smiles, and with a grimace, returns to stage right and sits on a rock. A few seconds. He stands up, sits on the ground, leaning against the rock. His hands around his knees and his head on his arms. The sound of a fife continues to be heard offstage. The boy raises his head and looks ahead, listening. Smiles. The boy looks around, stands up, smiles, and claps his hands once, taking one step forward limping. The fife stops playing.*)

BOY, (*furiously*).

Play…play, play, don't stop. (*Silence. Reflects and suddenly he gets furious, turning toward far stage.*) Play, play, don't stop. (*Thoughtfully.*) How beautiful it would be to see its face and not only to hear its sound! (*The sound of the fife starts again. The boy smiles. The fife plays for a few seconds and stops again. Violently.*) Hey…you miserable creature…play more, don't stop.

OLD MAN (*comes into light from the darkness of far stage holding a fife. He has white hair and white beard. Smiling. For shoes, he has rags wrapped around his feet. He wears rags with holes and gloves with his fingers showing*). Hey, there you are.

BOY. (*Remains in his position.*) Old Man, you came early.

OLD MAN. You're very romantic.

BOY. There is not such word is there?

47

OLD MAN. There was, but time has come and taken it away.

BOY, (*reflecting*). Yes, away to nowhere. (*Smiles and walks toward the Old Man, painfully limping.*)

OLD MAN. Why are you limping? Did you break a leg?

BOY. No, my shoes hurt me. (*Sits on the rock and, takes his shoes off and puts them on the ground.*)

OLD MAN (*picks up the shoes and examines them. Looks at them at all sides.*) Two right shoes. (*Puts them on the ground and looks at them again.*) They cheated you.

BOY, (*indifferent*). They're old.

OLD MAN. Then they cheated them.

(*Pause.*)

BOY. What time is it?

OLD MAN. It's too early yet.

BOY, (*violently*). What time is it?

OLD MAN. Look at the sun.

BOY. (*Stands up, one step forward, raises his head, looks, and immediately he lowers his head, wipes his eyes, raises his head again, shading his eyes with his hand. Turns, looks at the Old Man, sags over the Old Man, and speaks decisively.*) You're right. It's too early yet.

OLD MAN, (*after a short pause*). We always come too early. But still… it's too late.

BOY. It's too late for what?

OLD MAN, (*interrogatively*). Ah?

BOY. It's too late for what?

OLD MAN (*thoughtfully*). It's too late for…(after reflection)…for change, I suppose.

BOY. Don't think of change.

OLD MAN. You very well know, I never think.

BOY. Did you think?

OLD MAN. No.

BOY. Did you think of change?

OLD MAN. No.

BOY. Do you ever think?
OLD MAN. No.

(*Pause.*)

BOY. Then we'll never do.
OLD MAN. It's a condition of life.

(*Pause.*)

BOY. There is nothing to be done.
OLD MAN. Nothing?
BOY. Nothing
OLD MAN. We'll see.
BOY. When?
OLD MAN. Tonight.

(*Pause.*)

BOY. Do you have something in mind?
OLD MAN. Mind!
BOY. Ah. (*Silence. Picks up the fife, raises it in front of his eyes. He looks at it, smiles.*)
　　　　At least, we have something.
OLD MAN. The only thing left.
BOY. It's something though.
OLD MAN. It's something among nothing.
BOY. Can you define nothingness?
OLD MAN, (*after a short pause*). Look around.
BOY, (looks around). I see nothing
OLD MAN. There you are.

(*Pause.*)

BOY, (*picks up the fife and looks at it*). Old Man, do you remember when I was a little boy?

OLD MAN. No.
BOY.

>You used to take me by the hand down to the river, to make me a fife. Do you remember?

OLD MAN. There is nothing to remember.
BOY. I used to break every single one and…
OLD MAN, (*interrupts*). Yes, you were always like that.
BOY. And the next day, we went again down to the river to make me a new one.
OLD MAN. There were a lot of reeds then.
BOY, (after a small pause). Will you make me one now?
OLD MAN. There are no more.
BOY (questioningly). No more?
OLD MAN (*after a small pause*). No more reeds.
BOY (*after a silence*). Old Man?
OLD MAN. Yes?
BOY. Will we go down to that river again?
OLD MAN. No.
BOY. Then tell me a story.
OLD MAN. I told you all I knew.
BOY. Tell me a new one.
OLD MAN.

>We'll have a new story tomorrow. (*Pause.*) We always have a new story after a new day.

BOY. What about today?
OLD MAN. It's the same one I told you yesterday.
BOY. You never told me a story yesterday.
OLD MAN. Then the day before.
BOY. You didn't then either.
OLD MAN, (*agitated*). Then last year…three years ago…when… when we were on that dead lake.
BOY. Tell me that one.
OLD MAN. I forgot it. (*Starts to stand up.*)

(*Pause.*)

Boy. Old Man?

Old Man (*getting angry*). What is it?

Boy. Why were you taking me to the dead lake?

Old Man. To kill the time.

Boy. Will we go again?

Old Man. It's too far away.

Boy. We can walk, can't we?

Old Man. How are your feet?

Boy. Not worse.

Old Man. How's your back?

Boy. Not better.

Old Man. Do you feel pain?

Boy. As usual.

Old Man. Then you're alive.

(*Pause.*)

Boy. Will we go again?

Old Man. Where?

Boy. To the dead lake.

Old Man. What for?

Boy. To kill the time.

(Pause.)

Old Man. It's too far away. We'll kill it on the way.

Boy. Then we can't

Old Man, (*sits under the makeshift tent and wraps a blanket around him*).

What did you do before you came here?

Boy. I inspected the cages.

Old Man. How are the rats?

Boy. The same.

Old Man. Any changes?

Boy. The newborn open their eyes.

Old Man. Did they die?

BOY. No.
OLD MAN. Then things are getting worse.

(*Pause.*)

BOY. It's getting cold.
OLD MAN. The sun is setting. Get a blanket.
BOY. You have one on your shoulders.
OLD MAN.
>Ah, that's mine. (*Takes the blanket from his shoulders, he folds it, and puts it beside him.*) Have you brought the flints?

BOY. There are no more flints.
OLD MAN. There are no more flints? What happened to the river, to the seashore?
BOY. They're dead.
OLD MAN. How can we light the fire?
BOY. We can't.
OLD MAN. The night will come.
BOY. We can't stop it. It's a law.
OLD MAN. Yes, it's a law. (*Silence.*) It's a natural law.
BOY. Is it a natural law?
OLD MAN. Yes. The only thing left.
BOY. What nature?
OLD MAN. No the law.

(*Pause.*)

BOY (*walks toward far stage*). I'm getting cold.
OLD MAN. Do you expect to get warmth from the stars?
BOY. It's not possible.
OLD MAN. You'll freeze to death.
BOY. I have a blanket.
OLD MAN. Then you won't.

(*Pause.*)

Boy. I'll go and get my blanket.
Old Man (*abstractly*). What did you say?
Boy. I'll go and get my blanket. (He doesn't move.)
Old Man (nervously). Well, go.
Boy. No. I'll wait.
Old Man. For what?
Boy. For the sun to come down.
Old Man. It *will* come down. You can't stop it. It's a…
Boy (*interrupting*): It's a natural law.
Old Man. Precisely.

(*Pause.*)

Old Man. Do you feel cold?
Boy. I wouldn't feel cold if I had a blanket.
Old Man. You have a blanket.
Boy. Yes.
Old Man. Then go and get it.
Boy. But what about later on?
Old Man. What about it?
Boy. I'll need two.
Old Man. How do you know?
Boy. I always need two when the sun falls.
Old Man. You never had two.
Boy (*after reflection*). Yes, I never had two.

(*Pause.*)

Boy (*pointing at the blanket*). Is that your blanket?
Old Man. From habit.
Boy, (*violently*). *Is that your blanket?*
Old Man (looking for it). Apparently.
Boy, (after a small pause). Will you share it with me?
Old Man. *Mine…* I mean, that blanket?
Boy. Yes.
Old Man. No.

BOY. I'll be cold.
OLD MAN (*idiotically*). What did you say?
BOY. I'll be cold.
OLD MAN. Ah!
BOY. And then…(*pause, hesitates*). Will you share it with me?
OLD MAN. And you'll also share yours with me?
BOY. Yes. (Delightedly) Then we'll have two.

(*Pause.*)

OLD MAN. No.
BOY, (*questioningly*). No?
OLD MAN. No.
BOY. I'll die.
OLD MAN. Then I will.
BOY. Why don't you let me die?
OLD MAN. Because I have to explain.
BOY. Explain? Explain what?
OLD MAN. About the rats.

(*Pause.*)

OLD MAN. Go now. It's getting late. The night will fall.
BOY. Yes, the night.
OLD MAN, (*sings*).
> The night is a nightdress
> Which falls and covers all…
> Go now. Go…go.
BOY. Where?
OLD MAN. Anywhere but go, go…and come back before the night falls.
BOY. I'm going (exits stage left).
OLD MAN, (*sings*).
> The night is a nightdress
> Which falls and covers all

The things, which are more or less
Too big to fall and roll.

(*Noise of things falling offstage. The Old Man turns and looks toward stage left. Continues to sing.*)

One day I went to see
The rising of the sun...
OLD MAN, (*turns toward stage left*). Hurry, hurry.
BOY, (*offstage singing*). And I never had the chance.
OLD MAN, (*singing*).
The moonlight scandalizes
The small and hanging stars;
(*Out of tone*)
Entangling in their nets
The mellifluous men.
BOY, (*enters stage left with closed eyes and his hands behind his back. By the time the Old Man finishes his song the boy has reached him and stumbles on him. Steps back and opens his eyes looking at the Old Man frightened*). I'm sorry.
OLD MAN. What is the matter with you?
BOY. I'm sorry I had my eyes closed.
OLD MAN. You must always have your eyes open.
BOY. I didn't...
OLD MAN, (*interrupting*). Did you bring your blanket?
BOY. I didn't mean...
OLD MAN, (*interrupting violently*). Did you bring your blanket?
BOY, (*abstractly*). The blanket...(*seriously*) Oh, yes of course the blanket.
OLD MAN. Did you bring it?
BOY. (*With an idiotic smile, he reveals the blanket from behind his back*) Yes.
OLD MAN. Let me see. (*Takes the blanket and examines it.*) What colour is it?
BOY. It used to be green.
OLD MAN. Is it not now?

Boy. Not anymore.

Old Man, (*after a short pause, he throws the blanket to the ground*).
Well, it makes no difference. It's still a blanket.

Boy.
Yes, it is. After all, you cannot see its colour at night. (*Short pause.*) I always use it when the sun falls. (*He sits down.*)

(*Pause.*)

Boy (*thoughtfully*). Life.

Old Man. What?

Boy, (*thoughtfully*). Life, what about life?

Old Man. What about it?

Boy. Isn't there any order in it?

Old Man. No, there isn't any.

Boy.
But we feel the cold, the pain, we are hungry, we see light and darkness…we expect night after day.

Old Man.
Then there is. (*Pause. After reflection.*) Night. You just mentioned night. Didn't you just mention night?

Boy. I don't remember.

Old Man. *Yes, you did.*

Boy. And what if I did?

Old Man. Did you?

Boy. I suppose so.

Old Man. We always suppose.

(*Pause.*)

Boy. What is going to happen at night?

Old Man. Wait and see.

(*Pause. The lights fail slightly. The Old Man and the Boy lie down one foot apart and get under their blankets. They close their eyes. Silence. A few moments. The Boy raises his head and looks at the Old Man.*)

BOY. Old Man, are you sleeping?

OLD MAN. I can't.

BOY. Will you share your blanket with me later on?

OLD MAN. Yes, later on. The time hasn't come yet. Go to sleep.

BOY.

        Of course, it hasn't come yet. I'll go to sleep. (*Leans down again. Silence. The Boy raises his head again after a moment.*) Old Man, are you asleep yet?

OLD MAN (*violently*). *I can't.*

BOY (*idiotically*). Will you share your blanket with me if I fall asleep?

OLD MAN (*angrily*). If I'm awake.

BOY, (*leans down again. Silence. Raises his head again after a moment*).

Old Man? (*The Old Man doesn't answer.*) Old Man, can you hear me?

OLD MAN (*very angrily*). Yes, the only thing I can do!

BOY. Are you sleeping?

OLD MAN (*violently*). If you let me, I will.

BOY. When will the exact time be?

OLD MAN (*exploding*). There is no exact time!

BOY. It's already dark.

OLD MAN. Not yet completely. (*Violently.*) Will you let me sleep?

(*Pause.*)

(*Boy gets up and starts walking up and down the stage noisily.*)

OLD MAN (*raises his head, looks at the place where the Boy was laying, notices he's not there, turns to the other side. He sees the Boy and says violently*). Go to sleep and let me sleep in peace.

BOY (*jokingly serious*). I can't, I'm afraid.

OLD MAN. Afraid? Afraid of what?

BOY.

If I lean down... I'll fall asleep, I'll get cold, and you won't share your blanket with me...because you'll be sleeping and then...(*idiotically*)...and then I'll die.

OLD MAN. Plainly idiotic.

(*The Boy continues to walk noisily. The Old Man reflects, gives up, gets up, folds his blanket, and sits on it.*)

OLD MAN (*crosses his legs*). All right, I won't sleep.

BOY (*smiles, goes, and stands in front of him*).

It's very kind of you. (*Looks at him for a while, reflects, smiles, then walks toward his blanket, unfolds it, and speaks seriously without looking at the Old Man.*) I'll go to sleep. (*Gets under the blanket.*)

OLD MAN (*stands up, goes near the Boy, and kicks him on the ribs, violently*).

I didn't get up just for you to go to sleep. I got up because you wouldn't let me sleep.

BOY. I'm not stopping you. Go to sleep if you want to.

OLD MAN. No, I won't.

BOY. Don't you want to sleep?

OLD MAN, (*angrily*). No. (Goes and sits on the rock.)

BOY. Why?

OLD MAN (*angrily*). Because I'll fall asleep...

BOY (*interrupting*). And you won't share your blanket with me...and I'll get cold...and I'll die.

OLD MAN. Precisely.

BOY, (*stands up, folds his blanket, and sits on it. Silence. Looks forward abstractly. Turns his head, looks at the Old Man, turns forward, stays motionless for a moment, then turns again, looks at the Old Man for a while, and turns forward again. Stays motionless for a moment, speak gently*). Is it the time yet?

OLD MAN (*after a short pause, abstractly*). Ah...the time.

BOY. Time.

OLD MAN (*same*). The *exact time*?

BOY. Yes.

OLD MAN (*same*). No.

(*Pause.*)

BOY (*sadly*). Tell me a story.
OLD MAN. What story?
BOY. Any story. (*Short pause.*) About the rats.
OLD MAN. Not yet.
BOY, (*bends his head, stays motionless, and looks rather abstract. While in that position, he puts his hands into his trouser pockets, first in the right one, then in the left one, finds nothing. He tries on his shirt, finds no pockets, he gives up. A few moments, stays motionless, reflects. At that position, he speaks abstractly*).

> The story of the rats. (*Short pause.*) It's a ridiculous title. (*Short pause. Turns to the Old Man.*) Will you tell me the story of the rats? (*Silence. The Old Man does not reply. The Boy bends his head and says in comical imitation.*) Not yet. (*Short pause. Turns his head to the Old Man and speaks lyrically.*) Do you have a certain time to tell me the story of the rats?

OLD MAN (*softly*). Don't spoil it.
BOY. The story?
OLD MAN (*silently*). The silence.
BOY (*after reflection*). Is that so important?
OLD MAN (*forcibly*). The tings which are difficult to find are always important.
BOY, (*mockingly*). Ah, is that so?
OLD MAN (*violently*). Yes, that's so.
BOY.

> Ah. (*Bends his head; a few seconds, looks at the Old Man, opens his mouth to say something, says nothing, smiles, and speaks in a very low voice.*) It's something which must be kept secret. (*Smiles, turns his head, looks around, then looks toward the auditorium, fixing his eyes at a certain point, stays motionless, reflects. Puts one hand on his waist and speaks in a soft madam's voice, rather comically.*) And now I'll tell you the story of the rats. (*Short pause. In his voice.*) Wrong.

(*Short pause. Puts his left hand in his pocket and his right hand under the armpit of his right arm. Speaks with a rude voice, looking toward the auditorium.*) And now I'll tell you the…(*looks at his left pocket; his hand is moving. Takes it out of his pocket. He holds a little stone. Looks at it, then throws it away. Goes back to his initial position and speaks in the same tone.*) And now I'll tell you the story of the rats…

OLD MAN (*violently*). *Shut up!*

BOY (*turns to the Old Man surprised, speaks angrily*). Is this something which must be kept secret?

OLD MAN (*coldly*). Let me be.

BOY (*lowers his hands, one step back, puts hands in his pockets, and he reflects. Walks toward stage right slowly, bending his head, and whistling. Three steps, turns his head, looks at the Old Man, smiles, reflects, turns, walks three steps, turns again, looks, smiles, reflects. Turns his head, stays motionless, looks at the Old Man, smiles, and reflects. He stays in this position for a moment. Speaks distinctly*).
I'm leaving. (*The Old Man doesn't respond.*) I said I'm leaving. (*The Old Man does not respond. The Boy turns again, four steps forward, stops turns, looks at the Old Man, smiles, reflects.*) I'm leaving.

OLD MAN (*coldly*). Well?

BOY (*after a silence*). Aren't you going to stop me?

OLD MAN (*after a silence*). You won't go far.

BOY (*turns his head and while he walks, smiling, he speaks with a comical expression*). And if I do?

OLD MAN. You won't go farther than the cages of the rats.

BOY (*stops, turns completely, and faces the Old Man, reflects. Thoughtfully*). I won't go there anymore.

OLD MAN. There is no other place to go.

BOY. I'll go to the dead lake.

OLD MAN. You'll get tired. It's too far away.

BOY (*turns his head toward the auditorium, reflects, sober*).
I can walk for days and days. (*Short pause.*) My feet feel better naked. (*Short pause. Turns to the Old Man.*) You can't come with me, Old Man.

OLD MAN. Then you can't find the dead lake.

BOY. I'll meet another old man who'll know where the dead lake is…

OLD MAN (*interrupting, laughs briefly*). You'll meet nobody.

BOY (*turns toward the auditorium, sober*).

>And I'll stay with him, waiting for that cold night to come…and I'll leave him. (*Short pause.*) But first, he'll promise me to tell me the story of the dead lake…(laughs briefly)…and…and…and then…and then he'll promise me to tell me the story of the rats…if he'll have any.

OLD MAN. The only thing left.

BOY (*turns to the Old Man. Abstractly*). What did you say?

OLD MAN. The only thing left.

BOY. What, the rats?

OLD MAN. No, the explanations.

BOY.

>Ah. (*Reflects, turns towards the auditorium. Sober.*) But he won't. (*Short pause.*) He'll never tell me a story. Any story. (*Reflects, turns to the Old Man. Speaks violently.*) You never told me a story, Old Man, any story.

OLD MAN. I don't have to tell you stories. You can feel.

BOY (*walks toward Old Man*). Nothing.

OLD MAN. You can smell.

BOY (*still walks*). Nothing.

OLD MAN. You can see.

BOY (*still walks*). Nothing.

OLD MAN. You can hear.

BOY (*stops*). Nothing! Nothing, nothing, nothing. What can I feel?

OLD MAN. The pain.

BOY (*with gesture*). Yes, since I got onto this mountain.

OLD MAN. More likely.

(*Pause.*)

BOY (*quietly*). I haven't seen the world in years.

OLD MAN. You don't need to see.

BOY (*looks at the Old Man, walks quickly toward him, stands above him, he bends his head over him*).

> Old Man, have you ever seen the world?

OLD MAN.

> You don't need to see it. (*Disgusted.*) You can smell it. Pooh! The stench left by humans.

BOY (*after a short pause*). Is it the time yet?

OLD MAN. More or less.

BOY (*violently*). Is it the time yet?

OLD MAN. It doesn't make any difference. It can be any time.

BOY (*turns his head and looks at the Old Man violently*). Any time for what?

OLD MAN. For the stars.

BOY. It must be dark though.

OLD MAN. More likely.

BOY (*reflects. After a short pause*). What did you say?

OLD MAN. I said it must be dark.

BOY. I said that.

OLD MAN. Did you?

BOY. Yes, I did.

OLD MAN. Well, why did you ask me then?

BOY. To tell me what *you* said.

OLD MAN. It'll change nothing.

(*Pause.*)

BOY (*stays motionless for a moment, reflects, turns, and sits on his folded blanket. He speaks coldly*).

> All right then, let's have it.

OLD MAN. We have nothing to have.

BOY. The talk… I mean *the talk*.

OLD MAN. Ah, the talk. Well. (*Silence.*)

BOY. Well.

OLD MAN (*after a pause*).

> Are you cold? (*Leaves the rock where he was sitting and comes and sits under the makeshift tent next to the Boy.*)

BOY (*exploding*). That's not the talk. I'm talking about what we were going to discuss.

OLD MAN (*after a short pause*). Are you cold?

BOY (*violently*). *No, I'm not. I'm burning.*

OLD MAN. Well then, the night hasn't come yet.

BOY (*violently*). What about the stars?

OLD MAN (*abstractly*). Ah!

BOY. The stars…the stars. What about the stars?

OLD MAN (*raises his head, looks at the stars, says in musical tones*). What about them?

BOY (*anxiously*). To have stars, we must have night. This is a…

OLD MAN, (*interrupting*).
This is a natural law. Yes. But I can't follow unnatural laws when there is nothing left…but these.

BOY. Well, we must follow some kind of laws, natural, or human.

OLD MAN. It's not absolute. The first humans didn't follow human laws.

BOY. They follow natural laws.

OLD MAN. That's true. Then they took their position against nature.

BOY. And what did they do?

OLD MAN. They created human laws. (*Short pause.*) And then… (hesitates).

BOY. And then?

OLD MAN. Here we are.

BOY. Where?

OLD MAN (*violently*). Can't you see?

BOY. I see nothing.

OLD MAN (*points stage right*). Look there.

BOY. It's dark.

OLD MAN (*points forward*). Look there.

BOY. It's dark

OLD MAN (*points up in the sky*). Look there.

BOY. I see stars.

OLD MAN (*with gesture*). That's all.

BOY. What's all?

OLD MAN. Stars.

BOY. Stars?

OLD MAN.

       Stars. Our life is like a star. You don't know when you are born, you don't know when you die…you don't know where you live. All you know is you…a sign…sinking somewhere indeterminate. You don't have the feeling of time, nor the feeling of life or death. You have the feeling of substitution, as a star.

BOY. Comfortable nothingness.

OLD MAN. Inscrutable darkness.

BOY. Inscrutable paths.

OLD MAN. Darkness.

BOY. Paths.

OLD MAN. Darkness.

BOY. Paths.

(*Pause.*)

OLD MAN. Pathetic.

BOY. Rheumatic.

OLD MAN. Neurotic.

BOY. Dogmatic.

OLD MAN. Poetic.

BOY. Lyric.

OLD MAN. Pathetic

BOY. Plethoric.

(*As they are reciting the lines above, their tones are getting higher and higher.*)

Boy, (*turns his head left, looks; turns it right, looks; turns it back, looks; stands up, walks toward stage left looking down passing his look through stage right and far back. Turns his back to the audience, walks toward far stage, disappears in the darkness of far stage; a few moments, comes back into light, walking toward the auditorium looking down. Goes and sits again on the folded blanket. A moment of reflection. Sighs anxiously).*

        There is nothing to be done. (*Makes a desperate gesture.*)

OLD MAN (*after a short pause*). Did you find anything?

BOY. Not a grain.

(*Pause.*)

OLD MAN. God doesn't exist.

BOY, (*after a silence*). What did you say?

OLD MAN. God doesn't exist.

BOY (*questioningly*). He doesn't exist?

OLD MAN. Only for the Israelites thousands of years ago.

BOY. Foolishness.

OLD MAN. Foolishness? Foolishness to exist only for them?

BOY. Foolishness to say so.

OLD MAN (*after a short pause*). A—

BOY (*interrupting*). What's the use of existing if we ignore our existence? (*Silence.*) How's he sup—

OLD MAN (*interrupts*). Who's *he*?

BOY (*abstractly*). God.

OLD MAN. Ah.

BOY. He…(*tries to get back to his speech*). If…(*reflects, turns to the Old Man*). What was I saying?

OLD MAN. When?

BOY. Just now.

OLD MAN. He. (*The Boy shakes his head in the negative.*) If?

BOY. If…no, no, before that.

OLD MAN. How's he—

BOY.

        Yes. How's he supposed to help people if he doesn't know who's who? (*Short pause.*) You leave your cradle as a child with expectations. You arrive at your grave creeping as a worm.

OLD MAN. And this, my boy, this is the expectation of man, I suppose?

Boy.

> To arrive at his grave, creeping as a worm. Yes. But before that, he'll call himself a "man." Comfortable nothingness.

(*Pause.*)

Boy. I'm hungry.
Old Man. Do you expect God to feed you?
Boy. I went to the river before I came here.
Old Man. Did you find anything?
Boy. Cans.
Old Man (*after a short pause*). Well?
Boy. Empty.
Old Man. Did you read the labels?
Boy. Carrots…corn…beans…peas.
Old Man. Empty?
Boy. One inch of sand.
Old Man. At least we have something to look at.
Boy. What?
Old Man.

> Sand. (*Short pause.*) If we start eating sand, someday, we'll shatter and we'll be surprised because we thought we were eating carrots and…corn and…and…and…peas.

Boy. You can distinguish the sand from the peas.
Old Man.

> Yes, but not the sand from the empty cans which are supposed to contain peas and corn and beans. (*After a short pause.*) Did you find anything here?

Boy. Not a grain.
Old Man. Manna is an old story.
Boy. True for those who still believe.
Old Man. Let them live with beliefs.
Boy (*after a long pause*). They maintain wrong beliefs, but they won't get far.
Old Man. Who won't get far?

Boy. The thief, the liar…the…sufferer.

Old Man. There is no place for them.

Boy. There is no justice.

Old Man.

> There is no justice for the thief and the liar, but there is some kind of justice for the sufferer.

Boy. What is that?

Old Man (*after reflection*). To suffer.

Boy. Plainly idiotic.

(*Pause.*)

(*The Old Man stands up, stays motionless. With a grimace of fatigue, he turns and walks toward stage right slowly.*)

Boy. Where are you going?

Old Man (*without turning*).

> I'll take a walk. I'm tired. (*He walks toward stage right. The Boy watches him sitting on his blanket. The Old Man stops looks at the sky, stays motionless, reflects; lowers his head, reflects; turns toward far stage and walks, disappearing in the darkness of far stage. The Boy stands up, walks toward Old Man's folded blanket, bends over it to take it. Steps are heard from far stage; he raises his head, he looks at the Old Man, who comes into light and quickly retreats to his blanket, sitting down. He looks at the Old Man. The Old Man walks toward the auditorium bending his head and speaks slowly and thoughtfully*). Not a soul. (*Pause. Looks around and up in the sky thoughtfully.*) Not even a light. They're gone. (*Surprised.*) What happened to them? (*Looks toward the auditorium, bends his head, looks persistently for a moment, then stands straight, turns to walk away toward stage left. One, two, three steps, stops; stays motionless, turns his head, looks at a point auditorium right, turns forward, stays motionless, a few moments, turns his head suddenly and walks to where he was before; three steps, looks at the Boy,*

reflects, smiles. Speaks thoughtfully.) Ah, there you are. (*Still looking.*) A source of light.

BOY. Quite lyrical.

OLD MAN. Thank you. (*Turns toward the auditorium delightedly.*) And I thought that would be all.

BOY. You never think.

OLD MAN (*turns to the Boy. Speaks with irony*). Tell me, young man. Have you ever thought?

BOY. You very well know young men never think.

OLD MAN (*same tone*).

Have you ever seen a tiny source of light in the endless desert of darkness…while you're sinking in there?

BOY. It never happened to me.

OLD MAN. You never look for it because you are sinking in the darkness.

(*Pause.*)

BOY. I think I'll go to sleep.

OLD MAN.

Sleep, sleep. (*Turns around, facing the auditorium. Speaks abstractly.*) Sleep. (*Laughs briefly.*) What do we do all day long? Sleep. (*Brief pause.*) And then at night, we go to bed. (*Pause. Turns again toward the auditorium right, smiles, reflects. The Boy stands up, picks up his blanket, walks quickly, picks up the Old Man's blanket, walks to centre stage, stops, he looks at the Old Man, unfolds the blankets, and throws them down. Looks at the Old Man again and quickly goes under the blankets, closes his eyes. During the Boy's attempt, the Old Man's sight is fixed at a point auditorium right. He speaks abstractly.*) I thought you mocked me the other night. I thought you would never appear again. (*Short pause.*) But there you are. (*Pause. Lowers his head, raises his right hand, and holds his chin. Thoughtfully.*) Is that a hope? It can't be. But again…what kind of a hope…when everything is… hopeless. (*Pause.*) They say that…(*corrects himself*). They *said* that when a new life arrives at this exaggeration of life…a…a star lights…a star lights somewhere in space. (*Pause. Reflects abstractly.*) But again…they said that…that, when a new life arrives in this wandering world…the light of a star goes out. (*Pause. Reflects.*) Is it true? (*Short pause.*) If…we…(*hesitates*), then… I mean… I mean…it can't be true. It can't be the only living creature in the whole world. But no. There are more…but it's dark and I can't see them. (*Long pause. Pacing.*) Someone said that darkness hides…the truth. (*Short pause.*) And someone else said that…darkness is everywhere. (*Pause.*) Well? (*Pause. Turns back, points toward far stage, where it's dark, looks toward the auditorium. Speaks louder.*) Look there. (*Turns and points toward stage left. The same.*) Look there. (*Turns and points toward stage right. The same.*) Look there. (*Turns toward stage left, walks faster than his usual walk pointing toward that direction as he walks. As soon as he reaches almost the end of the stage speaks violently.*) Look there. Darkness. (*Turns toward stage right walking slowly. Looks at the Boy sleeping. Points at the Boy.*) Look there. (*Goes above him, looks at him, and kicks him at the ribs.*)

BOY (*speaks in a pained manner but without moving or opening his eyes*). Oh.

OLD MAN (*still looks at him*).

Darkness. (Turns toward the auditorium violently). Darkness. (*Short pause, speaks in a softer manner.*) They were right. (*Turns furiously to the Boy and kicks him on the ribs violently.*) Wake up, wake up, I (hesitates).

BOY. (*He doesn't move or open his eyes. He interrupts Old Man sleepily.*) Let me sleep.

OLD MAN (*with agony*). I'll tell you the story of the rats.

BOY, (*sleepy*). Not now. Let me sleep.

OLD MAN. (*Kicks him again angrily.*) Wake up, I said, it's time for the real stories.

BOY (pokes his head from under the blanket). It's too late, go to sleep.

OLD MAN. Now? (*Laughs briefly.*) Now when everything is lost?

69

BOY. You can say that again. (*Pause. Open his eyes.*) You made me lose my sleep.

OLD MAN.

You'll never sleep again. No one will. (*Walks around the Boy who is still under the blankets. Speaks calmly.*) It's time for stories. At least we can make some sense out of this illusion of life. (*Walks around the Boy, making a complete circle. Stops, looks at him, smiles, reflects, then turns, and walks slowly toward stage right. He's about to reach the end of the stage. Stops, bends his head, then raises his head, and turns and looks at the Boy. Reflects, smiles, speaks loudly.*) Do you remember when you were a little boy? (*The Boy does not answer. The Old Man stays motionless, looks at the Boy, smiles, then he turns toward the auditorium. Speaks with prophetic relish rather abstractly.*) When he was a little boy, he found me...or rather I found him down by the river. (*Pause.*) Rubbish was all over the riverbed. (*Short pause.*) It was a dry riverbed...well...who can deny it. Everyone knows it was a dry riverbed. (*Short pause.*) Tiny flies were flying around, cockroaches were crawling all over the place and...(looks at the Boy. Turns toward the auditorium and speaks silently)...and he was dirty and small and hungry. (*Short pause.*) I took him and I brought him...was it up here? (*Stops, reflects, scratches his head. Speaks thoughtfully.*) To the dead lake. (*Short pause. Same.*) To the...(*reflects*)... to the...well...to some place.

BOY (*raises his head, looks at the Old Man, and speaks loudly*). To the rats.

OLD MAN (*questioningly*). Eh?

BOY (*the same*). To the rats, Old Man, to the rats.

OLD MAN.

Oh, yes, to the rats. (*Small pause.*) Well, after all, who can remember after so many years?

BOY (*raises his head looks at the Old Man and speaks calmly*).

To the rats, Old Man, it's so easy to remember.

OLD MAN. Yes, but it's so hard to distinguish.

Boy. To distinguish what?

Old Man. The rats from the river…the dead lake…the cities…and, and the mountains.

(*Pause.*)

Old Man. Do you remember what happened there?

Boy. I was very young.

Old Man (walking toward the Boy). Do you remember how they used to like you?

Boy. I was just a kid.

Old Man, (*standing over him*).
You were standing in front of them, and they were behind the bars and you were talking to them.

Boy. Standing in front of them?

Old Man. Yes.

Boy. Talking to them?

Old Man. Yes, yes.

Boy. And they were behind the bars?

Old Man. Oh yes, that's what I said.

Boy, (*loudly*). That's a terrible thing to say.

Old Man. Terrible?

Boy, (*loudly*). Terrible.

Old Man. Oh, you mean you could be behind the bars, I suppose.

Boy. That would be different.

Old Man.
But then the rats wouldn't stay and talk to you. (*Short pause.*) The trouble is…someone must stay behind the bars. Either you or…or the rats, for instance.

Boy. And this, Old Man, this is a law, I suppose?

Old Man. This is a condition of life.

Boy. To stay behind bars?

Old Man. To be there without knowing why. Like for instance, the rats.

Boy. They don't know why they are there?

OLD MAN. Perhaps they know. But one thing is sure: we don't know
why they are there.

BOY. Someone should know though.

OLD MAN.

Someone, yes. But do they know it? I mean, do they
know why they are there? And if they know why they are
there, is it what the others know?

BOY. I suppose so.

OLD MAN. I agree with you. But the fact is they don't agree.

BOY. To what they think?

OLD MAN. To what they believe.

(*Pause.*)

OLD MAN. You used to whistle to them. (*Short pause.*) You stood
there for hours.

BOY, (*sadly*). Enough.

OLD MAN. But you wouldn't feed them.

BOY (*sadly*). I said enough.

OLD MAN. I mean there was nothing to feed them.

BOY (*after reflection*). Not even water?

OLD MAN (*abstractly*). I don't remember.

BOY. Old Man, how did you get the rats?

OLD MAN.

They came. (*Short pause.*) One day, I woke up and I
saw them inside the cages. I didn't tell anybody; I didn't
ask how they came. I accepted them.

BOY. How many there were?

OLD MAN. I didn't count them.

BOY. Perhaps you didn't know.

OLD MAN. I didn't know how to count?

BOY. You didn't know if you had to count them.

(*Pause.*)
(*The Boy stands up, rolls up the blankets carefully, bends over his
head, and looks at the blankets motionless.*)

OLD MAN.

Aren't you going to sleep? (*The Boy doesn't answer. He remains motionless.*) Aren't you going to *sleep*? (*The Boy doesn't answer. Still motionless. The Old Man looks at him for a moment, then walks toward him, stands behind him, bends his head a little to look at him, first at the right side, then at the left side. The Boy, still motionless, looking down. The Old Man stands on his toes and bends over the Boy's shoulder to look down where the Boy is looking. Gives up, walks and stands beside him, bends more, looks, raises his head, looks at the Boy, bends again, looks persistently, then he gives up. He stands straight and looks at the Boy. Turns his back to the Boy and walks two steps toward the auditorium.*) You can't do anything now.

BOY, (*turns his head, looks at the Old Man who has his back to him. Speaks abstractly*). Nothing?

OLD MAN. Your attempt would be absurd.

BOY (*walks toward the Old Man and stands behind him*).

But the dead river and the dead lake are the only things we have left?

OLD MAN (*walks toward stage right*). Apparently.

BOY (*turns his head and follows the Old Man with his eyes. Speaks persuasively*). You mean...

OLD MAN (*interrupts*). Did you forget the rats? (*Still walking.*)

BOY (*interrogatively*). The rats?

OLD MAN (*stops walking, turns around. Speaks loudly*). Yes, the rats.

BOY (*speaks anxiously*). We can't forget them.

OLD MAN (*speaks judiciously*). You feel kinship, I suppose.

BOY. But still we're free.

OLD MAN. And they're not free.

BOY. Precisely.

OLD MAN. And *we are* free.

BOY. Accurately.

OLD MAN (*loudly*).

Tell me, young man. Can you go to the dead lake, can you stay up all night without sleeping, can you stay hungry for days and days? (*Violently.*) Can you make a fife?

73

BOY, (*despairingly*). No.
OLD MAN (*triumphantly*). There you are.

(*Pause.*)
(*The Boy and the Old Man stay motionless in their positions. They reflect. They are at either ends of the stage. The Boy faces the auditorium forty-five degrees to the right. The Old Man faces stage left. They bend their heads, reflect. Silence. The Old Man raises his head, looks at the Boy.*)

OLD MAN. (*Puts his hands in his pockets, bends his head a little, observing the Boy attentively; stands straight. A few steps forward, looks toward the east attentively. Speaks indifferently*). The sun will rise in a while.
BOY. As usual.
OLD MAN. And it will be light once more.
BOY (*the same*). It follows.

(*Pause.*)

OLD MAN (*stands straight, reflects, and then with his hands in his pockets walks toward the Boy. Speaks in raptures*). Do you remember when we were sitting beside the river?
BOY. There is nothing to remember. (*Sits down.*)
OLD MAN (*after a moment of bewilderment, speaks in raptures*).
    We were sitting on the rocks, listening to the water flowing down the river. (*Short pause. Stands above the Boy, looking at him. Then he walks away. The same.*) The grass was high and green; the trees were flourishing, and it was warm and…and bright. Do you remember?
BOY. One cannot remember if one cannot forget.
OLD MAN. You can't even remember what the grass looked like?
BOY (*raises his head violently*). I can't remember what that day looked like.
OLD MAN. Is that so?
BOY. Simple.

OLD MAN. To forget?

BOY (*calmly*). To remember the non-existent.

OLD MAN. Do you mean that day never existed?

BOY. I mean that day will never come back. (*Long pause.*) Did you go to that river again?

OLD MAN. I can't find it.

BOY. Did you go to any other river like that one?

OLD MAN. There aren't any.

BOY. What happened?

OLD MAN. Now it's too late. You can't distinguish anything. Everything is a formless mass.

BOY. Like the mountain.

OLD MAN. Precisely.

BOY. Then...(*looks around and hesitates*). Well, we'll see in the morning.

OLD MAN (walks toward the Boy. Speaks irritably). You'll see nothing.

BOY. Not even light?

OLD MAN. The only thing which gives some sort of meaning to life.

BOY. I don't understand.

OLD MAN. Use your senses.

BOY. They're useless.

OLD MAN. Then use your fantasy.

BOY. The only thing that keeps us alive.

OLD MAN. And you still remain.

(*Pause.*)

OLD MAN. (*By now he has reached the Boy. The Old Man stands over him. The Boy's chin is resting on his knees. The Old Man looks at him, reflects, smiles, opens his mouth to say something, he says nothing. Stretches his right arm to touch the Boy's head. He's about to reach it. Hesitates. Takes his hand back. Speaks in a low voice.*) Bear it, my boy; man is nothing but a handful of clay. (*He goes one step back, turns, and walks two steps toward the auditorium. Speaks afflictively. Aside.*) He came to life. (*Corrects himself.*) He came to light. They brought him.

They brought him to light. Earn it. (*Long pause.*) If the rats die. (*Louder.*) If the rats die. (*Short pause. Calmly.*) There is nothing left. (*Pause. Looks up, looks around, smiles, looks toward the audience, smiles, reflects. Speaks very loudly.*) And they told me to remain. (*Laughs.*) They told me to remain and they are going to die. (*Short pause. Speaks thoughtfully and calmly in a low voice.*) They're going to die. (*Pause. Turns around. Looks in every direction, and while he walks fast and nervously toward stage left, speaks loudly.*) Is there anybody there? (*Walks nervously toward stage right, speaks loudly.*) Is there anybody there? (*Walks toward far stage nervously, speaks very loudly.*) Is there anybody there? (*Walks farther into far stage, disappearing in the darkness. Speaks very loudly.*) Is there anybody there? (*A moment of silence. He enters the light from far stage, walking slowly. During the Old Man's last attempt, the Boy raised his head and watched the Old Man frightened. The Old Man stands, faces the audience, and speaks in a low and calm voice.*) Not even a soul. (*Short pause. Turns, looks at the Boy for a few moments, motionless.*) There is nothing to be done.

BOY (*in a low voice*). Nothing?

OLD MAN (*same*). Nothing.

(*Pause.*)

(*The Old Man turns, walks toward stage left, and passes the Boy. The Boy suddenly stands up and runs behind the Old Man. He gets ahold of the Old Man's right arm. The Old Man stops and looks at him, trying to free his arm. The Old Man takes a step forward and he's about to fall. He stands upright, looking at the Boy.*)

BOY (*speaks angrily and loudly*). You asked me to come here last night.

OLD MAN (*musically*). So I did.

BOY (*more agitated*). You asked me to come here and wait for the night.

OLD MAN (*indifferent*). We waited. Now it's gone.

BOY. Why, why? (*Looks at him sadly.*) You didn't let me sleep…

OLD MAN (*interrupting, indifferent*). Life goes on.

BOY (*same tone*). You didn't lend me your blanket and what I had to do was...

OLD MAN (*interrupting, indifferent*). Life goes on.

BOY (*same*).

> Simply to take it. (*Both open their mouths to say something. The Old Man says nothing. The Boy speaks in the same tone.*) I was cold, I was hungry, and...

OLD MAN (*interrupting, indifferent*). Life goes on.

BOY (*speaks calmly*). What did you say?

OLD MAN. Life goes on.

BOY. And for the rats?

OLD MAN. And for the rats.

(*Pause.*)

BOY. Are they going to be in their cages all their lives?

OLD MAN. It seems like it.

(*They separate. The Old Man walks toward stage left. The Boy stays motionless to his initial position looking forward abstractly. The Old Man turns and walks toward stage right; passes the Boy and while he walks away, speaks in a low voice.*)

OLD MAN.

> There is nothing to be done. (*Turns and faces the audience. His finger points upward.*) It appeared there. (*Short pause.*) It appeared just for a moment. (*Laughs briefly. Speaks louder.*) It fooled me. I thought it was him. (*Smiles. Speaks admiringly.*) Whoever he was. (*Short pause.*) But he was not strong...and disappeared with the first sunbeam. (*Looks down, puts his hands in his pockets, and speaks thoughtfully.*) Why? If he was strong...(hesitates)... I mean he had to stay forever. (*Pause. Turns and walks toward far stage and disappears in the darkness for a moment. Speaks loudly.*) It appeared in the darkness. (*Pause. Walks into the light quickly. Speaks anxiously.*) Is this how he's supposed to appear? (*Smiles. Calmly.*) Well (*with a gesture*). Perhaps he

was not strong. (*Goes and sits on stage centre. The Boy still in his last position. The Old Man makes himself comfortable. Speaks calmly.*) What's the use of expecting if nobody appears? (*Corrects himself.*) If nothing exists. (*Short pause.*) I waited all my life. What did I see? Dead lake, dead river, full of rubbish, and empty cans. Not even a soul. (*Reflects.*) And as a result (*smiles, comically*)…rats in the cages. (*A loud, brief laugh. Stands up, walks toward the Boy. He touches his shoulder.*) Are you going to stay with the rats?

BOY (*abstractly*). I'm tired.

OLD MAN (*stands behind the boy staring east. One can see a spot light high up stage right with a dim light around it getting stronger as if the sun is rising. Lyrically.*)

The first sunbeams. The sun will be up in a moment. (*Smiles.*) A new day is rising. (*Turns and looks at the Boy.*) Are you going to stay with the rats?

BOY (*after a short silence, speaks abstractly*). Why did we come here?

OLD MAN (*feebly*). Did you see the moon?

BOY (*sadly*). Tell me, why did we come here?

OLD MAN (*same tone*). Are you going to stay with the rats?

BOY (*same tone*). Is this why we came here? To ask me that?

OLD MAN (*speaks in a normal voice*). Did you see the moon?

BOY (*meditating*). The moon? (*Reflects.*)

No, I didn't. I mean… I… I didn't look for it. (*Short pause.*) After all, how could I? We were waiting to get dark.

OLD MAN. It got dark. Did you see it?

BOY (*low voice*). No.

OLD MAN. Did you see a sign?

BOY (*low voice*). Not even one.

OLD MAN (*walks away*). Then I can't answer.

BOY. And what if I did?

OLD MAN. Did you?

BOY. I mean…let's assume I saw the moon.

OLD MAN. We assume all our lives.

BOY (*exploding*). Then tell me what is it?

OLD MAN. Nothing.

THE RATS

(Silence. The Boy looks at the Old Man while he looks at the audience.)

OLD MAN.

Are you going to stay with the rats? (*The Boy stays motionless for a moment. Without replying, he exits stage left. The Old Man doesn't notice. Speaks, looking forward.*) Are you going to stay with the rats? (*Silence. Turns around, notices the Boy is gone, turns forward, and faces the audience.*) Good. (*Pause. Reflects, then slowly goes and sits under the makeshift tent. Speaks timidly.*) I'm still remaining… (*short pause. The sound of the fife is heard offstage. Wearily*)… in the obscurity. (*Short pause.*) The rats are still remaining in their cages. (*Looks toward the east. The sun starts to rise. A spotlight slowly illuminates the Old Man while the rest of the stage lights go out slowly.*) And the sun rises once more. (*Pause. Animated.*) The light comes once more… and it will be dark once more. (*Short pause.*) Once again. (*Short pause.*) Light…darkness…light. (*Corrects himself.*) Darkness…light…darkness. And again darkness. (*Short pause.*) There is nothing to be done. (*Corrects himself.*) To remain but shadows. (*He repeats chanting.*) There is nothing to remain but shadows. (*Pause.*) Even…(*timidly*). Except (*short pause*). I came while it was light. I'm leaving in the light. (*Lyrically.*) Life is just a hope. (*Short pause.*) We'd come to light, hoping, we leave the cradle hoping. (*Short pause.*) We enter the darkness…(*corrects himself. Louder*). We enter the chaos, hoping…(*calmer*)…and still we say… I hope to death. (*Forcibly.*) Chaos! (*Exploding.*) Hoping. (*Exploding.*) Chaos. (*Thoughtfully and calmly*)… and…one step from the chaos is…the abyss. (*Mocking. Calmly.*) Hope. (*Stays motionless with a cold smile. Brief tableau. The spotlight goes out slowly. The stage is dark. The lights of the auditorium go on. The fife keeps on playing even after the lights go on in the auditorium.*)

ABOUT THE AUTHOR

Peter Routis has spent his youth in Athens, Greece, and his entire adult life in the Greater Toronto Area Canada. He has received his degree in English literature from Wilfred Laurier University in Waterloo, Ontario. He has written a number of plays, among them the *Tragedy of Eli* and the *Tragedy of Job* as well as *The Rats*, which, with piercing insight, Peter Routis illuminates the brutal and unavoidable destruction of the earth from climate change. Other works under various stages of drafts include "An Anthology of Poetry," "An Anthology of Short Stories," two plays, and a novel. A citizen of Canada as well as of Greece, Routis now lives in Newmarket, Ontario.

CPSIA information can be obtained
at www.ICGtesting.com
Printed in the USA
LVHW010308110719
623734LV00001B/7/P

9 781645 695806